Crossing the Mirror Line

JUDITH WILLSON

Crossing the Mirror Line

CARCANET

First published in Great Britain in 2017 by
Carcanet Press Ltd
Alliance House, 30 Cross Street
Manchester M2 7AQ
www.carcanet.co.uk

A CIP catalogue record for this book is available from the British Library.
ISBN 978 1 78410 499 3

The publisher acknowledges financial assistance from Arts Council England.

Typeset in England by XL Publishing Services, Exmouth
Printed and bound in England by SRP Ltd, Exeter

Contents

Noctilucent   7

Views in a landscape mirror

It's like that first winter morning   11
Mare Island   12
The commerce of snow   13
Views in a landscape mirror   15
The beautiful science of geometry at the
Ute Mountain Hotel   21
Dutch angles   22
The invasion of China   23
At Spurn Point   25
Julie's boat is in the field behind my house   26
Neither near nor far away   27
Slivovitz   31
Kleinvlei   32
Deer Shelter Skyspace   33

Reading the storm glass

Extracts from three humorous stories in which citizens laugh
    at the small troubles of their lives   37
Some favourable effects on bird life of the bombardment of
    our cities   38
The footnotes   39
Tales from a land of mountains remote from the great
    military roads   40
Two faces under a hat   41
Common Things Explained   43
Emptying the drawer   44
'George', painted as Lazarus   45

'Child 98', painted as his daughter Mary sleeping 46
In the garden shed, Yetta 47
When Yetta's mother is asked 48
Yetta listens to the house at night 49
When Yetta sleeps 50
Reading the storm glass 51

Keys, lightly touched

Watching a nineteenth-century film in the twenty-first century 55
Keys, lightly touched 56
'Day by day, good day' 59
A pencil draws a line across a ground 61
The alchemy of circumstance and chemistry in five photographs 66
The years before 68
Amateur magician 69
A bone flute 70
An optical experiment 71
Ink lines for Agnes Martin 72
All this 75

Notes 77
Acknowledgements 79

Noctilucent

We cross the garden: late sun, evening's slack tide.
He is remembering woods below San Pietro, the ragged end of a war.
Soldier and red-cloaked shepherd meeting on the road,
the old man calling his dog, waiting in the white road.
He watches how it goes on happening, the time it takes
to wade knee-deep in dazzle
towards the soft chalk curve between the trees.
The red cloak burned in his eyes. His hand, unsure.

He says *If a person walking raises his hand*
he sees the shadow of each finger doubled.

Trees slide down to lap us, attentive to our solitudes
until the hollow dark is filled with memory of light –
fluorescence, phosphor glow, poppies' slow burn.
Ghostlights to guide our double-going.

VIEWS IN A LANDSCAPE MIRROR

It's like that first winter morning

when you notice in the traffic
that tails down the valley, two – three –
bright cars with snow on their roofs

and you can't help looking up
to catch a rumour of pines and amber
and great bronze bells in a tower

above the two hundred steps of a citadel
where evening fall-winds stir sparks
out of dragon clawed braziers

and an owl's call carries the distance
from dark pooling under a forest
to first lilac light on the snowfields.

Sometimes we think this is how it could be.
How we think, sometimes, that it is.

Mare Island

each building had left behind only the history of its impermanence
Brooks Roddan, *Mare Island*

The white mare breaking loose – a constellation in flight
leaping clear from a ship, then she's running with the breakers,
her eyes wild for green. *Yegua blanca* the caballeros shouting
yegua blanca, *O beauty* streaming into the wind,
into the deafening light. Isla de la Yegua, Mare Island:

dazzle breaking over a bowsprit, speckle noise,
words for an island. Words for deerskin, bone earring,
for smallpox, glinting in deep-water channels.
No known word for green. You will say *shadow like leaves*
where fennel grows tall in welding shops, dry docks.

Five hundred ships – *Prometheus*, *Jupiter*, the destroyers,
Swift Boats that went down the Mekong into fields of water –
the Pacific closing over them, the white horses running.
A mare grazing in shadows of leaves, leaves shadowing the sea.
Passing further and further inside all its broken mirrors.

The commerce of snow

The eighteenth century was the Age of the Commerce of Snow
Information board on the icehouse, Val d'Alcalá, Valencia

Today the clerks are counting raisins
in our harbour warehouses.

> *Of Denia raisins cured in lye.*
> *Of Sir Joseph Hodges' raisins.*
> *Of raisins of Alicant, of Marabella.*
> *Of raisins entered at the customs house*
> *as raisins of Belvadera.*

Their fingers are gummy on the ledgers,
their tongues have thickened.
The sea is hard and blue. It does not move
our painted boats.

*

High above our syrup afternoons
snow-farmers rake their windrows. Day by day
they tread the harvest in our winter granaries.
Every glittering spikelet burns to the bone.
Every day is sealed in ash and straw.
The air is silver.

Soon the ice carriers will come to us
clattering down tracks in the night,
pines jumping scared at their shouts.
Their lanterns blink across our fever dreams.
Cold stars turn and turn in a slow minuet
down all the allées of our shuttered rooms.

Winter will shine in our mouths.
We will mouth it

like the dry rivers of Alcalá
streaming with snow melt.

★

In the harbour warehouses
clerks work on Sundry Accounts.
They disclose each transaction's symmetry –
so lucid, so distinct – catching its fall
through horizonless hours:
Received and Payable.

They scratch across the pages
like crows on winter hillsides

> *Of moon-cold lemon water for a quinsy.*
> *Of frosted grapes for Doña Ana's wedding.*
> *Of bonito pouring silver from the purse net*
> *into barrels packed with snow. Of ice.*
> *Of treasuries of ice.*

★

What prospects in our high dim rooms, what lustres
in our heavens! Our estates unfurl like silk.
In the streets, our carts and flags and running boys
revolve in perfect order.

The cobbles gleam, rimmed in silver.

Slabs of ice drip under sacking. Glistening runnels
creep, divide. Under benches where the creditors wait
beside a warehouse wall, last year's harvest
trickles towards the harbour.

The blue sea hardly stirs.

Views in a landscape mirror

Where the objects are great and near, the landscape mirror removes them to a due distance, and shows them in the soft colours of nature.
Thomas West, Guide to the Lakes, 1778

Principles of Linear Perspective (I)

(i) This uneven world is strung with invisible wires
tuned to perfection.

(ii) A beam of light will be pulled inexorably down
to earth's stone-blind centre.

(iii) A man who sets off on a long walk can be seen
becoming smaller and smaller
until he passes through
the Vanishing Point.

(iv) All this is beautiful and, if done correctly,
your picture may hardly be distinguished from the real thing.

Fragile as old film, the miners whistle their names' thin tunes –
John Newton, Cageman. Tom Evans, Shaftman – lines of them
rising from the archives, red dust on their backs. The youngest

have not grown into their clothes. No one lifts a latch
or sets foot in the parlour (*John Crellin? George Walker?*)
of the replica cottage entered through the replica mineshaft

where everything that happens has already, noiselessly, happened.
We could live here we think, comforted and quiet, mending
and making in the hearth's sepia light. *Very small,*

full of history, someone has written in the visitors' book.
We walk out to level sunlight, bleached air, pebbledashed streets.
A seawall curving away, a loading pier buried in slagfall.

'This peaceful nature reserve is not natural'

Here you follow the map. Keep to access paths.
Discover the home of the Scheduled Species,
the natterjack toad, the tern. Look for marsh orchids,
their mauve alchemical flame hissing in grass
as they break through the silica crust.
                                        Stand here,
meshed in invisible highlines and gantries,
in air full of skylarks pulling upwards rung by rung.

And under your feet, stacked vaults and shafts,
sealed workings where the sea plucks, sliding coils
gliding in silence perhaps, *with unfettered sweep*
through black windroads.
                            It is relentless,
the convergence of sightlines you walk through
between quarry and saltmarsh. Twice a day
unhistoried tides leave the mudflats rippled and shining.

A nice sharp boy

On 19th September 1903 Richard John Welch (age 13), began his fourth shift at No. 6 pit.

He worked on the wagons with Arthur Bond (age 14).

The boys' work was to pick stones out of wagons loaded with iron ore.

As a rule, the wagons stopped for 3 or 4 minutes under the hoppers.

Sometimes the boys would leap from one wagon to another while they were moving.

Sometimes they would swing from a plank and drop into a wagon as it passed.

They were told not to do these things, but they did them.

When the boys were nicely set on the wagons, the foreman waved off the locomotive.

Arthur Bond saw Richard John Welch clinging to a hopper.

Oh my waistcoat is caught.

Arthur Bond saw Richard John Welch fall between the last two wagons.

He saw two wheels go over him. He had warned him the day before

He had not to go in that place. He'd be getting lamed if he went in that place.

When Richard John Welch saw his father (Henry Welch, miner)

he called out *I'm done for now* (' – or something like that, Sir').

The foreman said the Deceased was a nice sharp boy
but he disobeyed rules.
No blame attached. He had not to go in that place.

Most awful and sublime

What was always remarked upon:
the slippery ladders
the guttering candle
the damp close air
its weight in the ears
the vast abyss
the dreadful majesty of the furnace
the consuming dark.

Now this place is a mirror to itself.
Wind has space to turn and roll,
the estuary is flooded with it.

Principles of Linear Perspective (II)

The man walking his dog through Red Hills once spent a summer
sketching the ironworks. You couldn't describe it, he says,

the circles of walkways climbing No. 1 furnace, the ladles' slow roll
swinging back empty on their chains.

How they raised the furnace door, how they gave him dark blue glasses
and what he saw was nothing that had horizon or measure.

How they lowered the door like an eyelid.
When he opens his notebook now he finds sinter on its pages.

Look, and his arm swings up the long diagonal rise of a kite
that's lifting away from a boy who plays its shrill line

to the wind, feeling towards the true point
where it all comes together. Each of us growing smaller

and smaller as it pulls up, holds taut at the apex. The drop,
everything flying apart very fast. The dog running, tide coming in.

The beautiful science of geometry at the Ute Mountain Hotel

A third-floor corridor, a bright vacant space I step into –
suddenly *fresco*, a white loggia, two gesturing figures
stilled to its measure. I the attendant, placed so to lead your eye

to the woman in a brown hotel overall, her arm raised,
washing windows. Who sweeps a dripping sponge
across Sleeping Ute Mountain, through a triangle of light that widens

from the parking lot out to the freeway. Who stops, and turns.
Over there, that's Shiprock. I live there. You can't see it in the dust
but after rain. Everything shines then. Oh it shines. Everything, then.

Each of us held at our exact and certain distance.
The shower unfolds its arc across the glass. For one moment
every drop of water encloses a tiny sun.

Dutch angles

a staircase / riser by riser   chambered / in sealight
    diamond bevel of a mirror   tangents of a clavichord
      her lace collar a white delta   his sleeve's allotted bounds
        the globe / her candle's transit   an empire / his hand's breadth

        the window / mirror a dominion   the mirror / window a horizon
     slipper askew / chequered tiles   chessboard / queen's move
   he / finger crooked to thumb   she / finger laid on mouth
a guilder spun on a table   a glass tipped below stairs

    my nutmeg my ivory / he   my sable my saffron / she
      my sandalwood my silk / he   my broadcloth my clove / she
        sea roads mapped on the palm   transactions of glances tallied
        calculus of tides / their treasuries   of gilded waters / a reckoning

The invasion of China

*In 1573 Captain Diego de Artieda petitioned the King of Spain for permission
to lead an invasion force of eighty men to China.*

Each horseman is a horseman's shadow. He watches the flickering line
he mapped on a sea of grass. Grey hills flow down the sky,

a bone-white mountain floats on inky clouds. *This is China.*
He wants to fill China's empty house with clocks and mirrors,

madonnas, cannon, pikemen. He wants his ship heavy in the water,
all China in its hold: *This is China, Sir!*

*It spins gold thread so fine a cloak will not fill your palm.
Its word for 'kingdom' means 'a wall enclosing jade'.*

*Its alphabet has six thousand letters, Sir. When it speaks
its words are pearls – are diamonds – falling in a silver bowl.*

Each horseman's shadow steps weightless through the grass.
China scrolls out ahead like weather widening across the plain.

★

The magistrate turns a mountain in his hand. He walks here
each evening, finding out its twisting paths. He names cliffs

and ridges, attends peaks that hang like breaking waves.
An ice-green river scarfs between his fingers.

A drift of rain falls through the wind. He thinks of his son
watching horizons darken like abandoned rooms below his lookout,

snow heaping thickly round the frontier post,
the passes closed. How he will stamp his boots, turn to the fire.

The mountain curls away like smoke. He lights a lamp
and sees a ripe moon hang lightly in his quince tree –

the world is not so large; a quince is not so small.
He picks up his brush, begins to write a path across the snow.

At Spurn Point

Dunes run into wind; sea has broken the locks, drags back
what water has made. Soon this place will be pared to a splinter

jagging at the mind's soft folds – crash of bells
in a drowned church at night, *the moon swallowed up,*

the North Sea tipped on end pouring through the chancel.
Monks' prayers, small broken boats. *Have you left it too late?*

You must stop here. A sign at the high-tide shelter
three miles from from anywhere that holds long enough

for light to settle. You must believe you will be safe
shallow breathing in your cedar-planked ark through hours

that seep into every cold space in your bones,
pull you so far from land that when the sea lets you go

you will find a new coastline humming in the haze – at last
a place you belong, where no one speaks your language

and none of the road signs make sense. The sound mirror tilts
its moon lens four minutes to the future. Returns with the tide.

It holds the estuary in its dish: the insistent faint pulse
of names on old maps. The rumble of incoming sea.

Julie's boat is in the field behind my house

A gale's punched the sheets on the line all day, now they're fighting
    out of my arms
to get back to the brawl and there's Julie's boat on the field crest
goose-winging into the slap of rain, prow sheering high
over a hawthorn reef.

In fog it's the *Flying Dutchman* ghosting its searoads down to the Cape.
Hikers walk at an off-kilter list to their dry-land bearings for the rest
    of the day;
passengers on the late bus rounding the corner are lost,
signal lights flashing unanswered.

And on winter evenings it's *Endurance* hung with frost-smoke,
circling inexorably in the Weddell Sea. The crew count out matches,
stare at lights in windows ten thousand miles north.
Hussey plays the banjo.

But today, in the clear light of rain, Julie's boat is in the field behind
    my house
like the word *boat* in Basque, singular in an ocean of words for boats,
lapped by a grassy swell calling its sea-name –
txalupa, txalupa, txalupa.

Neither near nor far away

per il mar senz'onde e senza lidi,
le péste né vicine né lontane.

Giovanni Pascoli, 'Nella nebbia'

You are thinking about hens,
how they bubble like kettles,
how they hitch up their skirts
and scuttle like busy women.

Your grey sisters whisper
you must not be disturbed.
Your good household women.

Hens with their old red eyes,
their sideways calculations.
They do not miss a single grain of maize,
scrabbling like women in the market
who have only one coin left.

How long ago
a circle of girls in the evening, heads bent,
tearing open papery husks, songs
thrown and caught in a ring. The maize
amber, swollen with milk.

How long ago
the night a grey mare trotted home
through the worn-out smell of August roads,
her reins trailing,
a dead man hanging over the saddle.

There was always a secret road to a green wood.
Always fathers and brothers were watching.

★

This is your life without words,
your caterpillar life
that eats at the starry green light
in your mind's tight-folded heart.

Sour kitchen smells, vinegar and lentils,
pig-killing winters, the village blood and dung.
A body hung and emptied like an old coat.
The tongue cut out and salted.

Winter was a room under a low roof
where your mother lay silent,
distinguished in her carved marriage bed,
slowly travelling out of her bones.

Your sisters wore jet beads,
filled your bowl with soup. Yellow pork fat
like the comfort of candles.
Your good grey women.

*

Old men on trams in quiet northern towns
carry boxes of cakes on Sunday mornings.
In the hills, their villages are empty,
streets curl in the sun like cats
round a church and a plane tree,

an alley into someone's courtyard
tangled in ropes and broken crates,
a window to a neighbour's storeroom.
Sacks of chestnuts and lentils for the winter.

A grey mare passed this way on a hot August night.

They knew the man who came home
hung over the saddle like the deer
fathers and brothers would shoot in the woods
where women picked strawberries
and girls walked arm in arm after work.

They knew his neighbour
who has not yet come home.

You buy cakes for your sisters on Sunday mornings,
read Virgil in the evenings. On hot August nights
you sit on your balcony, watch swallows
dart over the square until dark.
Leaves rattle in the fountain's dry basin.

Your father rides his grey mare home
and your mother waits, saying *How late it is,*
I heard the last train pass hours ago.

*

A man leaves and does not return
and nothing changes. Or
a man leaves and does not return
and everything changes.

Hens scratching dust in the maize stubble,
girls idling home from the fields.
Sheep brought down from the hills,
their bulging yellow eyes.
The village locked in its hunger.

All night the dogs bark at something
that leaves its stink in the orchard.
Fathers and brothers will go to the woods.
They know the paths, the trampled grass,
the torn branches.

Old women know how the story is told.
They keep it in a linen bag
filled with lavender and rue.
Never cut bread with a knife.
Drip olive oil into water.
Watch the little planets roll,
grassy gold as lamps in windows.

The shirt she gave him is white.
It hangs on a hedge, arms spread,
heavy with night mist.

★

How long ago
a grey mare and a white road.
A locked room. A story
that always begins in late summer
in ripe maize, the crackle of husks.
Girls' voices sing you through a green wood.
Their feet leave no prints.

And one day the swallows are gone,
the swifts have fallen silent. All summer
they never touched the ground.
A man's face becomes transparent as old linen.

You sit here with your book
in a small resort on a blue October evening,
thinking about hens.
The restless sea gnaws at the harbour.
Strings of coloured lights flap in the rising wind.
A boy shuts the café door.

Slivovitz

It's the kind of day – rain, disappointment, foot snagged
on barbed wire – when people decide to lay land drains,
phone a fencing contractor, get back on a level

because out there, humped tussocks of moorgrass
will twist like startled beasts to bite anyone walking,
black used-up fields slide over sandstone,

sandstone grates over mudstone and the wind is frantic –
where is birch, where is alder, where is the threshold?
Four generations worn to bone trying to haul it all in

to their keeping cellars, dragging causeys and walls
in their fists. Coping stones and heartings broken
rubble we've stumbled over. Quartz grit scattered in peat.

That house we knew we couldn't live in, a back wall
held up on acrow props all winter. János next door
grabbing a rabbit one Sunday morning, its squeals;

the slivovitz he made from our plums – farm gone in '57,
a silence on the lip of each glass. That taste, hard and raw,
the fallen roof of the barn he would never repair.

Kleinvlei

The stars are turning back across the hills; the small birds scatter –
a burst of sparks. An empty tree. A plane heading north
fades into morning.

Abram asks *How does a pilot find his way when he flies in the dark?*
The river twists down its channel, carrying a valley
grain by grain on its back.

In Kleinvlei women were singing *God is our everlasting rock*, water
braided over water. We passed through their voices
leaving no trace, like fish.

Deer Shelter Skyspace

Yorkshire Sculpture Park

Temple, lake, deer shelter triangulate Arcadia's vanishing point.
Leaves skitter in the empty summerhouse; beyond the sliding water
shadows herd beneath the arches of the shelter.

★

Walk into a concrete silo open to the sky.
There's nothing to see here.
What does nothing look like?

Flying over the curve of the Painted Desert, air opening like water,
barrel-rolling over fathomless sky in Pyramid Lake; farm lights at
    night far-flung as stars.
At dawn, the hangar shining: a memory of sunlight on a wall.

★

7.30am: linen laid over the valley; a gold bead; a glass bell.
1pm: ragged pennants; vapour swags; rinsed shorelines.
5pm: damson stain; smoke feathers; ink.

That this is nothing – how do we live with this?
We stare like deer into the event of light.

READING THE STORM GLASS

Extracts from three humorous stories
in which citizens laugh at the small troubles of
their lives

But Yakov had hidden his identity card in his boot!
Out of the crowd came a man with hands like spades.
For ten minutes he dragged Yakov round the floor
and the crowd was silent, watching.
Yakov cried *Comrades* before he closed his eyes.
The man pulled him up then flung him down again.
Get a piece of wood to keep him still he shouted.

★

They always sat together at an empty table in the canteen.
They corresponded by means of short notes.
I want to be in the country with you, eating cherries.
A poet once wrote that love comes when you fall
and someone falls down with you.
Kolya slipped and fell, dragging someone down with him!
The streets that day were bright with April sunshine.

★

Before the Revolution I lived with my aunt.
She owned a bicycle workshop near the station. *Chekhov*
she used to say, *is out of date now.* When I returned
I brought her violets and an electric kettle with a yellow flex.
She said *Don't let the Committee find out!*
I have to tell her I have been transferred to Kalinin District.
The fast train doesn't stop there.

Some favourable effects on bird life of the bombardment of our cities

Wrynecks were constantly heard around British Headquarters
during discussions of aerodromes. Swallows looped over the lake.
I watched the salients of their swerves, scribbled on a memo
The destruction of the human population
is no longer such a remote contingency as it used to seem.

There's a blackbird and a throstle sing on every green tree

I never discuss Allocation of Tonnage or movements of ships
outside this room. I track swifts' perfected migrations,
the flight patterns of lapwing; I scan winter skies for starlings,
wait for their sideslip over ministry buildings.
I follow dancing parties of goldfinches on frivolous excursions.

and the larks sing so melodious, sing so melodious

I do not entirely trust the Civil Service. Shortages of bacon and milk
may have caused a curious habit newly observed in bluetits –
papers shredded, notices ripped. *Bombing, favourable effects of,*
I slot into the card index between *Birmingham* and *Bradford.*
Starlings are roosting now among the anti-aircraft guns.

and the larks sing so melodious at the break of the day

I write *The disappearance of the human race from these islands*
would perhaps most inconvenience the lesser whitethroat.
A blackbird clamours brazen, jubilant, jubilant,
fireweed and cinders, a shattered hedge.
I shall persist in calling the song thrush a throstle.

The footnotes

After the wars, their monuments:
the heaped-up volumes – accounts of years,
minutes, the treaties. *Insofar as. At 3am. Unavailing.*[1]
The special character of the People.[2]
This document is unsigned. See Appendix.[3]
Has no recollection.[4] Work of diligent housewives,
winter coats they'd put away
in vast mahogany wardrobes for a season.
(*Ach, wax polish. That apartment in the Old Town.*)

You might open a door,
reach through thick folds into pockets
for a letter or a glove; something crumpled and dry.

1. *Our New Friends*, a first reader
   from the year before language reform.
   Bunches of keys. Loose change. A train ticket.

2. A pun on the word *strawberry*
   in the mountain dialect. Hand flicks
   for yes/no. Lace. A fondness for talking birds.

3. Postcards from the last exhibition
   of the Watercolour Society. Old jokes
   disrespectful to the chief of police. Irregular verbs.

4. A porcelain coffee pot, three cups,
   four saucers; doll-sized. Rosebud cups
   rimmed with gold, each saucer crimped like a leaf.

   No one any idea where or who
   by the time they were mine. Once, in a shop
   close to a bankrupt border I saw a matching cup
   in a box of screwdrivers, teaspoons,
   old beads. A quiet morning, sun in the streets
   and someone's leavings. The warmth going out of them.

Tales from a land of mountains remote from the great military roads

At last she had nothing left, and then…
Jacob and Wilhelm Grimm, *Kinder- und Hausmärchen*

There was once a poor woodcutter. Or there was a miller
or a tailor, and a daughter meek as curd. *And then?*

And then night with its mouth at the window: Gretchen,
there is nothing left now but ash in the barley. Nothing now
Gretchen but the taste of wet earth and ice on the wind.

She walks in the crowd crossing the bridge by the mill,
climbing the track to the mountains. She carries only a name.

Once there were words to call the night home.
It would lay its head in my lap, lick honey from my fingers.
Now dark waits under the bridge with its questions.

The last bird sings in a thicket *So it was, so it was,*
they hid my white bones. Oh Gretchen, who now will find me?

She sees the last house like a lantern in the clearing.
She sees one blue shirt left to dry in the orchard.
Smoke hangs in the valley over small virtuous farms.

Then she follows the crowd running through the tree line:
the woman who hid three tall sons in her apron, running,

the clever girl who sewed her brother back into his skin,
running; running into wind dark and empty as a drum.
Night takes the shapes of their passing, holds them till dawn.

Two faces under a hat

Aquilegia vulgaris

doves at the fountain

and folly's flower

soldier's buttons and

naked lady's foot

hawkfoot, crowfoot

or lady's petticoat

old maid's basket or

baby's shoes, also

old granny's nightcap

and granny hoods

fool's caps, skullcaps

dolly's bonnets and

two faces under a hat

Columbine,

which is Our Lady's flower, her dove, her soft foot,
signifying modesty

which flower is like to five eagles that meet together
mantling the torn lamb

which strewn unto bed straw protects from barrenness
and jealousy

which seeds, women whisper, gathered at Lammas moon
provoke the descent of blood

which hath poison in its seeds and roots, which causeth
heart pains, breathlessness

which pretty flower the custom is to plant on graves

which flower's thick roots continue many years

Here we go again,

Donna Nina, Miss Franceschina, La Bella Diamantina,
sister Colombina in your grass gown, trampling the wild garlic

leading a miry dance in and out of woodland's half-light gauzes.
O there's tricks i' th' world, there's sliding panels, masks,

there's tumblers and fumbled catches under the hell trap –
snap that slapstick, Signor Alichino – ropes, counterweights

behind the fairy palace. You'll remember the mirror routine,
Columbine tells the little girls in party shoes, you'll remember,

when January rain wakes you, your window shaken open,
the black roads hissing, the track end at a flooded storm drain,

your breath beating its wings in your ribcage. You'll know
exactly who I am, exactly who you don't yet know you are.

Step across. You'll find my doves sip-sipping the dark water.
You'll find my black glittering seeds.

Common Things Explained

The afternoon is soot and wool, damp coal. In an attic room
the uncles are inventing a new century with pliers and tinfoil.
They are building a brass and rosewood camera
to photograph dreams, a seismograph that will measure tremors
in the heart. Once, sparks burst into tendrils of shining dust,
branched fast and high like beans. The room recomposed
silently to dusk. Fat blebs of mercury quiver on a flowered plate.

Downstairs the maid is reading *Common Things Explained*.
How a Candle Burns. The Lunar Cycle. The Human Body:
its constituents; its rate of growth from infancy. Time,
measured by a uniform progression of events.
Soon I will be told to leave. The Pendulum. Kaleidoscopes.
She walks through the dark house, lighting a trail of moons
to guide the furniture home. Winds the clocks and waits.

Emptying the drawer

Finding your own birth noted
in a green pocket diary.

Walking home through the wet park.
Noticing a new drift of mushrooms

(Amethyst Deceiver, say,
which is not poisonous
nor even inedible
but is known to absorb arsenic
from contaminated ground)

has assembled in the leafmould.
An attentive crowd,
faces invisible under their thick felt hoods.

'George', painted as Lazarus

Artist's mannequin, 18th century. Oak, lime wood, iron, hessian

All I saw.
Light pooled in stairwells, bricked-up doors.
Wax flowers like cheese. Do not ask for wonders.

Every night
I heard roots grow across walls, dreamed a path
through a moonlit forest, lights in windows, a greeting

but every step
led back to the rusted pump in a tenement court,
a stairwell, a bricked-up door. I have no wonders to tell.

Still they circle,
the little *perfectionnées* ribboned *à la mode*,
busy as their sisters the looms. *Tell us, tell us.*

Heads tilted
just so. Shiny eyes click clack. *Tell us.*
He buried me. He buried me because he could raise me,

my lord of the mahlstick.
I returned blackened and mute, log
the weight of a planet. Hungry for everything laundered

Oh sweet as the morn.
Now he fattens his costumes and cloths
with shadows I brought him. He gorges on shadows,

he crams.
He locks my grapple fingers in his, works softly,
alert as a molecatcher to snare what lives in the dark.

'Child 98', painted as his daughter Mary sleeping

Artist's mannequin, 19th century. Wood, metal, horsehair, stockinette;
papier mâché head

Child 98 jumps up on her long iron legs,
shakes off her smile. Kicks away her hollow pink head.
She's blank wood, flat stump. Spade Face

slides her linseed oil, fingerprint musk
under Mary's lead-white sheets. *Awake arise*
I'll pull out your eyes sings Spade Face.

The bed is quilted in snow; the child lies deep,
her skin titanium, zinc. Seven hard winters.
Where is the posy he arranged on her pillow?

Spade Face isn't telling. *I'll pull out your tongue*
then see what you can say. An icefall of damask
inches to the floorboards. *He loved me best*

whispers Spade Face. *He buttoned me into your nightdress*
ruffled with frost, laid your sheets on my shoulders
in two glassy folds. He gave me your blue eyes.

I was warm in your snow bed, Mary.
Your sugar bones couldn't have taken my weight.

In the garden shed, Yetta

made herself small as an eyelash, quiet
as the crocus corms cutting milk teeth

on the windowsill where sun
crossed the iron claw of a weeder

to the hook-beaked secateurs
to the door snapping to its lock.

She stood at the window
watched herself walk with her mother

counting magpies on the lawn
one for sorrow one for sorrow one for sorrow.

When Yetta's mother is asked

she says Thank you, I believe Yetta is pretending to be a child
while she waits. I think she is memorising my shoes and gloves,

the dust eclipse under my perfume bottle. She knows how to fold a letter
back into its envelope, how a folded handkerchief must be smoothed

over the envelope. Her fingers read broken things, she steals sugar,
fills her pockets with pebbles and keys. I watch her wade in green dusk

through undersea rooms. I watch her breathe herself out on a mirror.
Her eyes are winter wrens, she will not say what they have seen.

I think she will leave us soon, her wet hem dragging at her knees.
By then my daughter will have learnt how to be unhappy.

Yetta listens to the house at night

      scratching at corners, its fast heartbeat in the walls

a tremor

      crouched to spring clear through the cold fractures

where a room jolted

      dropped into new shapes. The wind rages its grief

salt-raw

      tearing stones from the sea. Yetta gathers the house

in her arms

      rocks it quiet as moss. A house could be a boat

dipping to its shape in the water.

      A boat, or a hare that jinks away through wet grass

peeling out of its skin.

When Yetta sleeps

she puts on her red coat
with the three coral beads
stitched into its lining

and walks into a city
where snow falls for years.
The streets are deserted.

Bridges fly through the night.
Out in distant suburbs
the last trains have stopped.

She hears wind drag its stick
along railings, someone
ring doorbells, click switches.

She hears her mother call
Little bird, little bird.
She walks light as blown glass.

Reading the storm glass

Changes in the liquid in your storm glass will forecast the weather...

The chemistry has curdled. This morning the liquid was clouded,
shot with jumping sparks.

Now a storm is picking up your treasured things and laughing.
The air rings in your ears as if stones had fallen minutes before

and would not stop falling. The sealed glass holds its breath.
The broken skin on your hands will not heal.

On days when crystals slump like dissolving sugar
you will write your name again and again on scraps of paper.

It will be the wrong answer every time. In this place
your alphabet is deceitful as a wishbone.

If your thick blood would only stop clotting you could stand
weightless and legible in the hot salt wind.

At the sting of polar air, your crystals will seed to cottongrass
trembling on a starved moor. Now you will be alone until spring

walking a basalt beach the length of the peninsula,
miles of birch forest at your back.

After six weeks you are scoured luminous as an aluminium bowl.
The sky is soft as ash and each day tastes of glacier water.

Sometimes there is nothing to see in the glass but a window
curled like a leaf, rocking a little in silvery liquid.

You in your blue dress watching the sky turn over the sea,
you know how light will wash through this room

smelling of mint and a change in the weather.
You know there are yellow pears in a dish on the table.

KEYS, LIGHTLY TOUCHED

Watching a nineteenth-century film in the twenty-first century

Adolphe, Mrs Whitley and Annie wait in the garden
still in an angle of sunlight
that will never reach through the bay window
or unsettle the shade congealing under the trees.

They take four steps to turn into the shadows
at the edge of their afternoon;
four steps wheeling past us – skirts swinging, coats flapping –
a breath's length away as we watch in their dark.

Their bodies are a shower of particle-scatter,
their footfall a trick of snapshooting time.
They flicker across the frame at twelve frames a second
for two seconds for ever
no sound escapes them:
Adolphe counting their steps – and turn –

a neighbour's shout, a laugh, a road beyond the hedge spooling out, out
into the smash and roar that's falling towards us.

Keys, lightly touched

Three pieces from György Kurtág's piano work 'Games'

Flowers We Are, Mere Flowers... (...embracing sounds)

at the bridge we joined hands

we walked until they [...]

we were not permitted to cross

and at the bridge they [...]

and at the bridge we [...]

at the bridge we joined hands
we lay in the meadow grass

Perpetuum mobile (objet trouvé)

when yellow leaves blow round the statues
    when girls in a playground run singing
        green branch green branch the gold gate is open

when vines catch fire on a hillside
    when night gathers under a river
        when yellow leaves blow round the statues

when bells spill silver over dark water
    when the chess players' tables are empty
        green branch green branch the gold gate is open

when girls' plaited hair is a skein of smoke
    when their swinging arms are a falling arch
        when yellow leaves blow round the statues

when a river is a song that swims under ice
    when yellow leaves blow
        when the gold gate is open

Scraps of a colinda melody – faintly recollected

the lamp is lit   come home
come home my nine sons

our mother calls   her voice
sharp as a star   O my fine boys

our father calls   a church bell
across the clearing   my mother

my father   we cannot step back
through the door of your ribs

we dip our rough heads to pools
smell shadows   hear light

sink under moss   winter blows
through the long bones of our legs

'Day by day, good day'
Peter Dreher's 5,000 paintings of an empty drinking glass

One idea I had ... was to paint an invisible picture.
Peter Dreher, 2012

He paints light every day and every day
he is astonished how light collects into a glass's shape
on a white table against a white wall.
I wanted to paint something usual, like a glass.
Not a brick. *A brick is too heavy.*
Tomorrow he will paint the glass he has never seen before,
the one that holds the pearl of a lightbulb, or late sun
caught like a moth, its wings folded to fit.

These are his quiet fixed hours, the days' passage
amassed: a glass, a white table, a white wall –
there must be a window, an airy room, a house
where someone makes coffee, cooks herring?
In Mannheim light scoured from too many directions,
tasted of brick dust. He was twelve
and floating. *When I was twenty-nine I built a house.*
I learned this was not the way to get home.

The glass hovers on its reflection. The table's horizon
is grey and tremulous. How did we not notice
those low distant hills across the puckered water?
How cold the morning light dredging the undertow
where tenements, the best department store, the planetarium
are burning. And in that avenue of lindens
a woman is pushing a barrow between splintered trees.
A boy runs beside her in a man's clumsy brown shoes.

Tomorrow a slow current will carry the glass
past the warm slubby wall and he will be astonished

a glass could be so gold-flecked and ashy, so full
with the hour when the schoolmaster's wife has settled the baby
and plays a gramophone record, closing her eyes.
He will paint the weight that falls across her lap.
It's good if the glass after a time goes out of the painting.
When did the room become so dark?

A pencil draws a line across a ground

This is a rough sketch done by an officer who was killed in the same attack I was wounded in. Please take care of this for me.
Letter from Montazah hospital, Alexandria, 1916

The sketch

The paper's tracked and pitted, border country
marked by what moved across it; dust and light.
What he had in his sights – holding a pencil
to take his bearings from the zero line, trained
to adjust to the Correction of the Moment –
left its grains in puckers of rough ground,
ripening in darkness. Adjust to the moment
and in low sun, shadows resolve fugitive contours
in a field never turned by the plough.

Graphite

Metallic earth; they sweated their fever in its coal.
The glittering stone; they tore themselves open on its diamond.
They dreamed its lustre under bitter vetch and tormentil,
ripped through veins, hacked it from bellies.

It marked sheep to their fells, could spring open a lock
or blacklead a grate. It greased a cannonball's scorch
through an infantry square. It was effective against colic.
It drew the limit of God's outstretched hand;

had men stripped and searched at the end of a shift,
had armed guards posted at Harrison's Level,
had Black Sal hunted down by dogs (it was said)
for stealing an ounce. It cost more than gold.

A week to dig through four feet of Skiddaw Lava,
a ninety-foot drop at Grand Pipe to a coffin level.
It is opaque. Slippery. Insoluble.

Condition report

Under a microscope paper becomes a tangled net,
a pencil line becomes a gleam of stippled fish
whose scales flick tarnished silver as they slip
through deeper water
where they become a winter field swept by hail
and then a cratered planet.

Provenance

/ EMBARKED / DISEMBARKED /
Gravesend / Suvla [the *Brighton Belle*, the *Robin Redbreast*]
Port Said / Basra [the *Grampian*, the *Kalyan*]
Basra / Alexandria [the *Varsova*, the *Gloucester Castle*]
TERMS OF SERVICE: DURATION OF WAR
the work of digging parties continued
throughout the day and the night. Continuing
sleet on the wind. Continuing enemy fire. Continuing
thunder, rain bursting open the salt flats,
bursting the parapets. *On continuous fatigue 36 hours*,
rifle bolts clogged, drowned in dugouts and sandhills.
DURATION OF WAR *digging till daylight*,
Suvla to Mudros
Mule Track to Gully Ravine
Sheikh Saad to Crofton's Mound
Beit Aiessa halfway to Twin Pimples. Digging
through the flood that swept away overcoats, water bottles,
Battalion and Company records, the sick and the dead.

Cleaning and repair

In the valley of the fort, of revetments and guardhouses:
foxglove and birch. Bracken foams over trial pits,
fills the gashed mouth of the adit at Grand Pipe.

On the salt flats at Suvla: Jerusalem thorn and sea holly;
cistus and thyme at Cape Helles. Paper tears, softens,
ragged leaves sink under winter rain

and then in the hills above Gully Ravine: crocuses,
honeysuckle, iris; at Beit Aiessa milk thistles and sorrel,
as in the garden of the cottage in Seathwaite

where the mine steward lived with his two loaded guns.
Roots finger-tip into trenches, crawl past the guards
in forbidden areas, draw tangles of light through stone.

The alchemy of circumstance and chemistry in five photographs

Tacita Dean's 'Blind Pan'

[Exile, no sun]
This is a photograph of twenty years. There are no people
in it, and no shadows. He carries this famine
on his back; he carries his country in his mouth
and it has no word in it for *home*, no proverb of forgetting.

[Antigone leading, dark clouds]
Walking under rain. *Who was your father?* Gunfire in villages,
dogs at the gates. What does her voice look like?
Like the weight of her coat. Like bread. Like *Take my hand,
walk in my footsteps.* No. *Who was your father?* Like rain.

[Furies, 'your steps are dark']
Forests run howling for water; air shredded, wingbeats.
She cannot look into the burning, curls under herself
as if she were unborn. *Walk in my footsteps.* Her hand.
He leads her over the border, into dark, out of sight.

[Colonus, just out of frame]
Halting. Halt where a spring overflowing a basin
returns his face to him in silver and sunlight slipping over the brim
through wet, open hands. He sees the place when he knows it.
No one can look directly at the sun.

[Light. End here]
It begins, *no way back*, in a dark room, something taking
the imprint of light. In this photograph are constellations,
musics, scribbled maps; our chancy travel across peopled time.
And there is no exposure long enough to make this visible.

The years before

That time my grandmother went to the sixpenny hop
in the years before they became the years before
Tom Baxter and Rabbity Dixon played through the night
longways and hands across down the middle turn
and *K-K-K-Katy* and *Haste to the Wedding*

     and oh how

Tom could play the birds out of the trees with that old concertina's
steady push and pull the intake of air on the swerve a pounce
every time on the button driving the tune in close circles
and Rabbity sharp as his traps to snare the beat
swirling the tambourine's silver starlings

     over and over

towards a room she walked into one afternoon
when Will ran into the kitchen *Come down to the shop*
You must come and see this there's a man here says he's a
and there among boxes of collars and gloves resting palm to palm
the day quietly folding its hours away she shook hands with a lion tamer

     and heard again

all that wild blaze reeling and swooping
heel and toe stamp turn about and back again and
Goodnight Ladies and oh *The Girl I Left Behind Me*
somewhere out in the forest rough music rising
in the year that was becoming the year before

Amateur magician

Learn these tricks for an amusement, but do not carry them into your everyday life.
J. Theobald, *The Amateur Magician*

I studied how to cut the Princess of Thebes into nine pieces
and pluck the Lady of Karnac to hover at my fingertips
over a flaming pit. They'd have danced back every time,
those flexuous girls, to catch the paper bouquets
I'd whisk from my gloves.

And then, Swallowing the Needle, the Knife through the Heart –
the trick is to leave no visible traces. Palm up palm down
here's a coin in your ear, here's your purse in my hand
before you knew it had gone. Your earring?
Watch me cut open this apple.

What followed came easy: the Riffle Shuffle, the Faro Shuffle,
the snap and fan of Lost Queens descending a staircase again, again,
all the false cuts, false dealing, the Criss Cross, the Switch.
I mastered the Ambitious Card; fumbled the Finger Break.
It would always be Double or Nothing.

And look, there's nothing between my hands, nothing up my sleeves –
only a length of silk ribbon I'll walk through, without a cut or a knot.
It's Expansion of Texture, that trick that makes nothing appear.
It's my gift.
I've left you my Vanishing Card.

A bone flute

made from the radius bone of a Whooper Swan wing c. 40,000 years ago

Swans flying in across the lagoon at dusk, muscled as horses;
sky filling with bells. The swans dip and rock, lanterns

on the grey water and we raise our phones' small lamps
as if we should honour the messengers returning at nightfall

to patient souls who stand beside cars with their children
in bright winter coats holding bags of grain,

provisioned for a journey. The swans lift their necks,
open the great doors of their wings. Our faces are fading

behind our white breath; a flute's seven feathery notes
still dissolving on the air. Mothers or sisters

walking towards us, hold out their hands.
They will sit with us, watch the hours swing round,

skeins streaming north. Soon the year's first sharp light
will sing in the bone. Soon they will take what they came for.

.

An optical experiment

Seeing is like hunting and like dreaming
James Elkins, *The Object Stares Back*

You were told to expect this, to lose yourself
tracking a line of footprints over the ridge.

They were yours. You knew this too, knew
they would close, step by step, behind you

though whether you were following or leading
that pursuit, you did not know. Only that you must walk

towards the one bright spill from a window
to write up your notes in a room where a pale girl sits –

her red dress, a white wall, then your eye
slipping slantwise over a threshold. A clearing,

a summons to the place appointed. Her face, ink
clouding through water. Her dress, glacier-green.

Conclude the eye demands completeness. Conclude
an image may remain for seventeen seconds on the retina.

Even longer. One day you will stand at the door,
see yourself crossing a snowfield. Leaving no tracks.

Ink lines for Agnes Martin

We need more and different flags

a flag for the Airstream trailer

| a blue woollen blanket | a red suitcase | a tin of clams |
| black pencil/red pencil | an 18-inch ruler | a rose |

a flag for the silent studio

| a grey stone (warm) | 50,000 dabs blue/ochre | a mountain |
| a white stone (cool) | 50,000 dabs rose/blue | a cloud |

a flag for the rented mesa

| a canvas windbreak | a brush one inch wide | a fence line |
| a roofless house | white grass/yellow truck | a song about sky |

a flag for the northern islands

| a steel knife-edge | a canvas sail | a gull's breastbone |
| a wake breaking open | an empty bay | brimful of ocean |

Falling blue

In the sailmaker's loft on Coenties Slip
she tilts a blue Plexiglass box in her hands
a hundred beads sift and slew making
unmaking a wave swells breaks and breaks.

Islands sway through the tide race channels
the line her boat draws holds and dissolves
Nothing but blue skies her favourite song
sun swinging by whistles *never so bright*.

The sea rocks in its net of coordinates
at night the waves are fretted gold and blue
they tilt to blue and gold then nothing shines
in this room nothing but blue falling blue.

Untitled 2004

her last drawing
       before she died aged ninety-two
three and a half
       by two and three-quarter inches
one zigzag
       sharp ink line
finding a way
       quarter inch by quarter inch
into a cactus
       growing up from the rim of its pot
in spiralling
       thick-fleshed pads
it is simple
       how a cactus grows from nothing
but need
       until the line stops mid-turn
picks up
       and she's tied it off in a loop although
this cactus
       could go on inching up tugging
its long coil
       of urgent molecules up
to the sun
       were it not for that closed black clasp

       your eye cannot pass through.

All this

This is where it all comes home to us, in the fetch of light
crossing the mirror line and only a row of concrete blocks

grounds us here in the estuary's level give and take now
the machinery miles down between Stavanger and Bergen

begins to heave the whole weight of the sea round. Long swells
heaping over the *Blessing of Burntisland* unroll through the firth

returning the mudflats to sky. We are stiltwalkers
on a shining skim where clouds bloom under our feet;

we sway on our quicksilver legs until we are scattered
and the sanderling sheer away overhead, wheel back

grey-white white-grey – a shower coming in off the sea.
All this. And sea urchins, *Echinocardium*, blown from the surf

like bubbles of bone: the amazed *O* of all we could lose.
Our weightless luck. Our brittle, spiky hearts.

Notes

'Mare Island': a naval shipyard in California from 1854 until it was closed in 1993.

'Views in a landscape mirror': 'This peaceful nature reserve is not natural' from Cumbria Tourism pamphlet *Heritage Walks in the Western Lake District*. 'Gliding in silence with unfettered sweep' from Wordsworth's sonnet sequence on the Duddon estuary. 'A nice sharp boy' is based on the inquest into the death of Richard John Welch as reported in the *Whitehaven News*, 8 October 1903.

'The invasion of China': the penultimate line echoes a line in a poem by a seventeenth-century poet, Wang Chi-Wu, which itself draws on an earlier source (trans. Robert Kotewall and Norman L. Smith in the *Penguin Book of Chinese Verse*, 1962).

'Neither near nor far away': the poem draws on Pascoli's imagery and is loosely based on his life (1855–1912), in particular the defining events of his childhood: his father's unsolved murder and the death of his mother. The epigraph from his poem 'In the fog', reads '[I could only hear] on that sea without waves or beaches, / footsteps neither near nor far away'.

'Deer Shelter Skyspace': a work by James Turrell at the Yorkshire Sculpture Park, created from an eighteenth-century deer shelter. The poem draws on Turrell's account of his experiences as a pilot in 'Greeting the Light: an interview with James Turrell', in *Works and Conversations* (www.conversations.org).

'Extracts from three humorous stories': inspired by text in the *Crocodile Album of Soviet Humour* (Pilot Press, 1943).

'Some favourable effects on bird life': some details adapted from E.M. Nicholson, *Birds and Men* (Collins, 1951). Italicised lines in stanzas 1, 3 and 4 are quotations from the book.

'Tales from a land of mountains…': from the preface to the Grimms' *Kinder- und Hausmärchen*.

'Keys, lightly touched': Kurtág's *Játékok* (*Games*) is a collection of short piano pieces, originally intended for children. 'Flowers We Are…' consists of seven notes. 'Perpetuum mobile' is created by running a hand up and down the keys. 'Green branch, green branch…' is my version of a line sung in a Hungarian children's game. A colinda is a traditional Christmas or winter solstice song.

'Day by day, good day': Lines in italic are from interviews with Peter Dreher in *Peter Dreher: Just Painting* (Occasional Papers, 2014).

'A pencil draws a line across a ground': the derivation of the placename Borrowdale is 'valley with a fort'.

'The alchemy of circumstance and chemistry': Tacita Dean's description of analogue photography in her book *Analogue: Drawings 1991–2006* (Steidl, 2006).

'Ink lines for Agnes Martin': the phrase 'We need more and different flags' from a text by Agnes Martin in Arne Glimcher, *Agnes Martin: Paintings, Writings, Remembrances* (Phaidon, 2012). 'The ocean full to the brim' from the artist in conversation, quoted in the same. 'Falling Blue', title of a painting by Agnes Martin.

Acknowledgements

Earlier versions of some of these poems have been published in *The Compass*, *Eborakon*, *The Fortnightly Review*, *PN Review*, *Poetry London*, *The Rialto*, *Stand*, and the Carcanet anthology *New Poetries VI*.

'A pencil draws a line across a ground' is for Ruth. 'All this' is for Clare and Don.

I'm grateful to the many people who have read individual poems and the manuscript at different stages; in particular, my thanks to Judy Brown, Carola Luther and Helen Tookey. To Michael Schmidt, my thanks for encouraging and editing. And to Paul, my thanks as always.